The Research Report Series of the Institute for Social Research is composed of significant reports published at the completion of a research project. These reports are generally prepared by the principal research investigators and are directed to selected users of this information. Research Reports are intended as technical documents which provide rapid dissemination of new knowledge resulting from ISR research.

RESEARCH REPORT SERIES, INSTITUTE FOR SOCIAL RESEARCH

Employee Ownership

Michael Conte
Arnold S. Tannenbaum
Donna McCulloch

Survey Research Center
Institute for Social Research
The University of Michigan

1981

ISR Code No. 9012

This technical assistance project was accomplished under
a grant from the Economic Development Administration of
the United States Department of Commerce. The statements,
findings, conclusions, recommendations, and other data in
this report are solely those of the grantee and/or its consultants
and do not necessarily reflect the views of the E.D.A.

Published in 1981 by:
The Institute for Social Research
The University of Michigan, Ann Arbor, Michigan

6 5 4 3 2 1
Manufactured in the United States of America

Broad access to property is fundamental to the American economic system. Throughout our history, there has been a steady growth of institutions especially designed to help the average citizen acquire and safeguard property of one sort or another. The early Homestead Acts, Federal Deposit Insurance Corporation, credit unions, cooperatives, aid to small business, and more recently minority enterprise ownership assistance are just a few examples of broadening the property base of "expanding ownership."

One of the most recent variations to emerge is the Employee Stock Ownership Plan, or ESOP, which permits employees to acquire up to 100 percent of the equity of the firm for which they work. This plan not only affords a real increase in property ownership for the workers as individuals, but also serves as an instrument for new corporate capital formation.

The transfer of ownership is accomplished by an ESOT (Employee Stock Ownership Trust), a separate entity designed to receive the stock, or give it to the employees, repay such loans as have been made to acquire the stock, and to act as agent for the corporation.

The ESOP/ESOT may have any number of objectives apart from stock transfer and management. It can raise new capital, enhance current pension trusts, develop second incomes for stockholder-workers, or pursue any other set of legitimate corporate objectives. The ESOP principle finds both interest and support among a wide variety of disciplines, from investment bankers to social scientists. Many students of the quality of working life perceive positive correlations between worker participation and productivity, between job satisfaction and the sharing of decision-making responsibilities.

Despite growing interest in expanded ownership in general, and ESOPs in particular, little organized research has been done. There are several success stories, to be sure, but appearances do not define causality.

EDA is the Federal agency most directly responsible for economic development in areas which suffer unemployment, underemployment, or sudden economic downturn. The Public Works and Economic Development Act of 1965, as amended, authorizes the use of various economic stimulants — public works assistance, business development and loan guarantees, research and development, technical assistance, and other special impact forms of aid.

The question has arisen whether newer forms of employee ownership, such as the ESOP-ESOT models, are reliable tools for redevelopment. Can failing business firms be saved? Will areas which have resisted other forms of development incentives be stimulated into growth and new work opportunities by expanded ownership devices?

EDA put these and other related questions to the Institute for Social Research of the University of Michigan. This report is their response and and represents, we believe, a pioneer effort. The study is divided into two parts. The first is a general overview and analysis of a variety of employee participation expanded ownership programs — including many ESOPs. The second part is a study of one specific ESOP, 100 percent of whose stock is owned by the employees.

The overall findings are necessarily tentative, particularly in the case of ESOPs included in the sample, whose history is too short for absolute conclusions to be drawn. Nevertheless, it appears that optimism would not be inappropriate, and that further study of long-term performance is warranted.

                    Office of Technical Assistance
                    Economic Development Administration

I. Employee Ownership

This section concerns firms that have adopted a plan of employee ownership. Employees at all levels in these firms own stock varying from a very small percent of the company's equity in some cases to as much as 100 percent in other cases. We have located 472 such firms. Ninety-eight were identified through information in newspapers, magazines, and professional journals, as well as through information provided by persons who are familiar with employee owned companies. In some of these companies employees own stock through an employee stock ownership trust (ESOT); in others employees own stock directly. The remaining 374 firms were identified through information provided by the Internal Revenue Service from applications by these firms for ESOT status.

We have collected detailed information in the first 98 of the above firms, including such information as industry type, number of employees, magnitude of sales volume, the percent of employees who participate in the ownership plan, the percent of equity owned by non-managerial as well as managerial persons, whether ownership is direct or through a trust, whether ownership implies voting rights and whether employee representatives are on the board of directors. We also measured the attitudes of managers toward the ownership plan and their judgment about the effect of the plan on productivity and profit. In thirty of the companies we were able to obtain actual data about profit, and we therefore analyzed for this sub set of companies the relationship between profit and some of the above aspects of ownership.

The data that we have collected along with the analyses that we have performed offer preliminary evidence concerning the possible impact of expanded ownership on the economic viability of firms and on their ability to save jobs.

Summary of Findings[1]

We estimate that more than a thousand firms in this country have some form of employee ownership plan (not including profit sharing and pension trusts), although in most of these firms the percent of equity owned by employees, particularly by non-managerial employees is small. We were able to identify and to collect data from 68 firms in which at least 50 percent of the equity is owned by employees. In 20 of these firms, non-managerial employees themselves own at least 50 percent of the equity either directly or through an employee stock ownership trust.

Managers offer a number of reasons for having established an employee ownership plan. The incentive that it provides to employees and the tax advantages that it affords the company were among the prominent reasons given by managers in firms with employee stock ownership trusts. Reasons that are related to the creation or maintenance of employment were also mentioned by some of the managers of ESOT firms, but these employment-related reasons were offered more frequently by managers of firms in which employees own stock directly.

Managers in both types of firms are in general very supportive of the ownership plan and they see the plan as contributing to the productivity and profit of the firm. In fact, the thirty firms in our sample for which data about profit are available do show a higher level of profit than do similar conventional firms in their industry, although it is not possible to assert on the basis of this comparison that employee owned firms in general are more profitable than conventional firms, since the firms in our sample may be select with respect to profit. It is clear, nonetheless, that employee

---

[1]This section of the report was prepared by Michael Conte and Arnold Tannenbaum.

owned firms can function efficiently and profitably. Furthermore, analyses concerning the possible determinants of profitability of these thirty companies indicate that the single most important correlate of profitability among the aspects of ownership that we measured is the percent of the company's equity owned by non-managerial employees. The greater this percent, the greater the profitability of the firm.

Introduction

Examples of expanded ownership can be found throughout the history of the United States. An unpublished survey, for example, has found that 389 firms in which a large proportion of the stock is directly owned by employees were established in this country between 1791 and 1940.[1]

Employee ownership can take two forms: direct, in which employees own shares in the company as would any shareholder in a joint-stock company; or "beneficial," in which employees own shares through a trust. Since the passage of the Employee Retirement and Income Security Act of 1975 (ERISA), the only type of trust which may legally accommodate large amounts of investment by employees in their company's stock is the Employee Stock Ownership Trust (ESOT).

Contributions to an Employee Stock Ownership Trust are governed by an Employee Stock Ownership Plan (ESOP) which requires that the trust invest primarily in employer securities, unlike a normal pension trust or profit-sharing trust which must diversify its holdings. The plan may leave the method of contribution entirely to the discretion of a single party or parties or it may specify one of several methods of contribution. Contributions may be made on the basis of a profit-sharing principle (whereby some fixed percentage of company profits is annually transferred to the trust), a cost principle (whereby a fixed percentage of labor costs is annually transferred to the ESOT), or a fixed contribution principle (whereby a fixed dollar amount is transferred to the trust). The central requirement, however, is that the ESOT invest "primarily" in employer securities, and that disbursements from

---

[1] Jones, D. The economics and industrial relations of producer cooperatives in the United States, 1790-1940, n.d.

the ESOT be made in employer securities. Dividends that may be declared are not usually distributed immediately to employees but rather are held in trust. Nonetheless, the financial well-being of the "beneficiaries" of stock in the ESOT is tied to the success of the company.

We include in this study data from both these types of plans but not from other types of stock ownership trust, such as profit-sharing and pension trusts. Under present law these latter trusts are not permitted to hold large blocks of employer's securities.[1]

Method of Selecting Companies for Study

We compiled a list of 148 companies in the United States and Canada that we thought might have some degree of employee ownership. This list was culled from articles in newspapers, magazines and professional journals, from conversations with colleagues, and finally, from references given by persons in employee-owned companies whom we contacted. A letter was written to the president of each of these companies, asking permission to conduct a fifteen to twenty minute telephone interview. These persons were generally willing to participate in our survey, although many of them delegated responsibility for the interview to another officer, usually a financial officer. Interviews were finally conducted in 132 companies, of which 98 actually proved to have some component of worker ownership. These 98 cases, seven of which are in Canada, serve as the main basis for the analysis of this section.

In addition to information about the above 98 companies, we obtained copies of recent applications to the Internal Revenue Service from 374 firms for ESOT status. These applications represent the work in progress in the 13 IRS key districts at the time of our request to the IRS. Some of the information included in the IRS records overlaps with information obtained through interviews with the 98 firms and a limited comparison can therefore be made between the

---

[1] For an analysis of some firms that have substantial profit sharing programs, see Profit sharing in 38 large companies, piece of action for 1,000,000 participants. Vols. 1 and 2. Evanston, Ill.: Profit Sharing Research Foundation.

two sets of firms. For example, 41 percent of the employees in the average firm of the IRS set participate in the ownership plan compared to 77 percent of the employees in the average firm of our first set. Our initial selection procedures, which were designed to locate firms with "substantial" employee ownership have understandably led to firms that have a higher participation rate for employees in ownership than the norm. The plants in this set, however, are comparable in size to those of the IRS set, the average number of employees in the former case being 1,448 compared to 1,334 in the latter.

Description of the Companies

Data from the IRS records. Table 1 presents data from the IRS applications that describe several features of ESOPs and that illustrate how ownership through an ESOT may differ from direct ownership. The vesting period is one such feature. Stock that is held in trust but is not yet vested to an employee may be forfeited if the employee leaves the company for reasons other than sickness or death. This condition, which applies to ESOPs, does not apply to direct ownership and, as the first two columns of Table 1 show, the vesting period in the average ESOT begins about three years after the employee has joined the plan and is completed seven years later. Large firms, however, may commence and complete the vesting process faster than small firms. (In some companies, the vesting period may be as long as 20 years.)

A second feature of ESOPs concerns the right of employees to sell their shares, which right they do not have until the shares have been "distributed" to the employees. Column 3 of Table 1 indicates that in 72 percent of the firms in the IRS "sample" distribution does not occur until after the employee leaves the company. This prevailing feature of ESOPs may not differ in principle from that in cases of direct ownership, where ownership of stock is a condition of employment.

Column 4 of Table 1 provides information about the basis upon which stock is allocated to employees. In 82 percent of the cases the amount of stock an employee receives is proportional to the employee's wage or salary, although the allocation formula need not be linear, and it may take into account other considerations, such as seniority.

Column 5 indicates that in some ESOP firms employees themselves must make a contribution toward the purchase of their stock, but this feature occurs in only seven percent of the ESOP firms in the IRS set. It may be somewhat more frequent in larger than in smaller firms.

Column 6 presents information concerning the percent of employees in each firm who participate in the plan. A larger proportion of employees participate in small firms compared to large ones.

Data from telephone interviews. Of the 98 companies where we interviewed a managerial representative, 68 have ESOPs and 30 have direct ownership. The firms differ a good deal from one another in number of employees, as shown in Table 2, although in general they are relatively large by conventional standards. Furthermore, ESOP firms in this set are larger than directly owned firms, even though both types include a broad distribution of size.

Size as measured by sales is presented in Table 3. Forty-five percent of the firms in our set had sales of at least $25,000,000.

Table 4 indicates that as many as 50 percent of the ESOP firms in our set are wholly owned by employees including managers while only 19 percent of the directly owned firms are wholly owned by employees. However, in 78 percent of the directly owned firms at least half of the equity is owned by employees. Table 5 shows the percent of equity owned by the ESOT. The percent of stock owned by workers themselves is, of course, lower than the above figures, as Table 6 indicates.

Table 1

Some Characteristics of ESOP Firms in the IRS Set

Size of Firm: (number of employees)	Average number years till vesting begins	Average number years till fully vested	% cases where "distribution" not allowed before termination of employment	% cases where allocations are made on basis of total compensation	% cases where employees must contribute	Average % of employees participating in ESOP
14-74 (N=100)*	3.5	10.8	75	86	0	77
75-149 (N=79)	3.2	10.2	71	90	2	68
150-424 (N=101)	3.2	10.2	81	82	2	58
425-46842 (N=94)	2.2	7.6	60	72	25	49
All (N=374)	3.0	9.7	72	82	7	62

*Number of cases

Table 2

Number of Employees in ESOP and Directly Owned Firms

Percent of Firms

Number of Employees	ESOP (N=68)	Direct Ownership (N=30)	All Firms (N=98)
4-99	18%	20%	18%
100-249	18	37	23
250-999	38	23	34
≥ 1000	26	20	25
Total	100%	100%	100%

Table 3

Sales Volume of ESOP and Directly Owned Firms

Percent of Firms

Sales (in millions of dollars)	ESOP (N=68)	Direct Ownership (N=31)	All Firms (N=97)
less than 1	6%	10%	8%
1-10	22	24	22
10-25	20	35	24
25-100	32	17	28
>100	20	14	18
Total	100%	100%	100%

Table 4

Distribution of Percent Total Equity Owned by Employees (including Managers)

	Percent of Firms		
Percent Total Equity Owned by Employees	ESOP (N=60)	Direct Ownership (N=27)	All firms (N=87)
< 9.9%	4%	4%	4%
10-49.9%	18	18	18
50-99.9%	28	59	38
100.0%	50	19	40
Total[*]	100%	100%	100%

---

[*]Eleven firms did not provide sufficient data to determine the percent of equity owned internally. They are eliminated from this table.

Table 5

Percent of the Firm's Equity Owned by the Employee Stock Ownership Trust

	N	Percent of Firms
Percent of equity owned by trust:		
0-9.9%	15	26%
10-24.9%	20	34
25-49.9%	11	19
50-100%	12	21
Total*	58	100%

*Ten firms did not provide data on the percent of equity owned by the trust.

Table 6

Percent Total Equity Owned by Workers

	Percent of Firms		
Percent Total Equity Owned by Workers	ESOP (N=58)	Direct Ownership (N=25)	All firms (N=83)
less than 3%	34%	8%	27%
3-9.9%	16	8	13
10-49.9%	43	20	36
50-100.0%	7	64	24
Total*	100%	100%	100%

* Fifteen firms did not provide data relevant to the percent of equity owned by workers. They are eliminated from this table.

A measure of equity owned by workers in each ESOP firm was obtained by multiplying the percent of the company's equity owned by the ESOT times the percent of the ESOT's equity owned by the workers. Because of the way records are kept in most of the ESOP firms, we found it necessary to rely on the distinction between salaried and non-salaried personnel as the basis for distinguishing rank-and-file workers from managers in these firms. Furthermore, while all of the respondents in the directly owned firms were able to provide information about the allocation of ownership between managers and non-managerial personnel, only about half of the respondents in the ESOT firms were able to provide precise information concerning the allocation of stock within the ESOT. In these firms, 54 percent of the ESOT stock on the average is owned by non-salaried employees and we assume that this average defines the amount of stock belonging to workers within each ESOT of the remaining cases.[1] The percent of total equity owned by workers in these remaining cases, as we estimate it, is therefore directly proportional to (i.e., 54 percent times) the percent of the company's equity in the ESOT itself.

Table 7, based on the above assumptions, provides information about the amount of equity owned by workers in firms of different size. Substantial ownership by workers occurs predominantly in firms of moderate size rather than in the very small or the very large ones. For example, workers own at least half of the equity in 42 percent of the firms having between 100 and 249 employees. By way of contrast, workers own this much equity in only 12 percent of the

---

[1] The definition of "worker" implicit in the above procedure differs somewhat in the two types of firms. "Worker" may include foremen and salaried clerical workers in some directly owned firms, but not in the ESOP firms. Table 6 may, therefore, overstate the difference in worker ownership between ESOP and directly owned firms, although we do not believe that the definitional inconsistency accounts for the entire difference shown in the table. Furthermore, we "control" for this variation in definition in the regression analyses shown below.

Table 7

Distribution of Percent Total Equity Owned by Workers in Firms of Different Size

Percent Equity Owned by Workers

Number Employees	0-2.9%	3-9.9%	10-49.9%	50-99.9%	Total
4-99	31%	13	44	12	100%
100-249	24%	15	29	42	100%
250-999	22%	19	37	22	100%
1000-18000	31%	16	37	16	100%
Total	27%	13	36	24	100%

firms of under 100 employees and in 16 percent of the firms of over 1,000 employees.

Reasons for Adopting Employee Ownership

Respondents were asked their reasons for adopting an employee ownership plan. Answers were classified as follows:

Incentive: e.g., "Ownership provides an incentive for employees to work harder" or Employees will be "more conscientious about their work."

Financial: e.g., "ESOP provides us with a tax advantage" or "ESOP permitted our company to raise needed capital."

Moral: e.g., "Employees should own part of the company that they work in."

Employment: e.g., "The company would have closed down if the employees had not bought it" or "It [employee ownership] is a good way to start a business."

Miscellaneous

Each respondent was permitted to indicate three reasons and Table 8 gives the percent who mentioned each of the above categories as one of their responses. While the "incentive" and "financial" motives appear to be the more prominent ones among the ESOP firms, "employment" stands out as a reason for the creation of the direct ownership plans.

The relative importance attached to financial reasons for the adoption of an ESOP undoubtedly reflects the tax incentives associated with ESOPs as well as other features of an ESOP that might prove advantageous under some circumstances. For example, the principal owners of a business may wish to divest themselves of their holdings while retaining control of the business. The owners can accomplish this through an ESOP in two ways: by passage of nonvoting stock to the ESOP or by passage of voting stock but not permitting "pass through" voting. In the latter case, the trustee of the ESOT, who may be accountable to the board of directors of the company rather than to the

Table 8

Reasons for Adopting Employee Ownership Plan

Percent of Firms[*]

	ESOP (N=68)	Direct Ownership (N=30)	All firms (N=98)
Incentive	41	13	32
Financial	37	0	25
Moral	12	7	10
Employment	12	53	24
Miscellaneous	53	43	50

[*] Percents are based on the total number of firms represented in each column and these percents add to more than 100 since respondents might provide more than one reason.

employees, may be entitled to vote the shares in the ESOT. By making one of these two arrangements, the principal stockholder in a closely held company can retain control over the company without actually holding a "controlling interest."

Ownership and Control

We asked two questions of respondents in ESOP firms in order to determine the extent to which voting rights are included along with ownership. (1) "Do the shares in the ESOT have a voting right which may be exercised by either the employee owner or the trustee, that is, does the ESOT hold voting stock?" (2) "Does the ESOT have pass-through voting, i.e., can the employees direct the trustees on how to vote the shares in the trust?" One question was asked about voting rights in directly owned firms: "Are employees entitled to vote if they own a share in the company?" The answers in response to these questions show a marked contrast between ESOP and directly owned firms. Of the 64 ESOPs which responded to the first question, 17 indicated that the stock in the ESOT is voting stock. On the other hand, of the 30 cases of direct ownership for which we obtained an answer to the relevant question, 29 companies indicated that employees who own shares in the company could vote their stock. In 28 of these cases, the vote is direct; in one, it is by proxy. Table 9 presents some of these data.

The large disparity between the answers from ESOP and directly owned companies indicates the complexity of the ownership concept. Ownership is essentially a set of rights. In legal terminology, two basic ownership rights are "right to corpus" and "right to control." Right to corpus permits the owner to sell the property that he or she owns and is usually associated with

Table 9

Voting Rights

	ESOP (N=64)	Direct (N=30)	All firms (N=93)
Can employees themselves vote, or direct the voting of the stock that they own?			
Yes	27%	97%	50%
No	73	3	50
Total	100%	100%	100%

a claim to all the profits generated by the property. Owners in an ESOT share in the capital gains and losses of their stock and are entitled to dispose of their stock once it has been distributed to them. Their ownership rights, however, generally do not include the right to vote their stock. Nonetheless, some control may be exercised by employees in other ways, such as through a union. Workers on the board of directors of the company, which is becoming increasingly popular in some European countries, is a further way in which employees might exercise influence in employee owned firms.

Companies with ESOPs and those with direct ownership do not differ greatly in the extent to which employees are unionized, as Table 10 indicates. About one third of the companies in both groups have some employees who are unionized. (We did not inquire about the extent of unionization within the company. It is our impression that directly owned companies have significantly fewer unionized employees than do comparable ESOP companies.) Large differences are apparent in the table, however, when it comes to other measures of employee influence over company decisions. For example, 36 percent of the respondents in companies with ESOPs report that worker representatives sit on the board of directors, while 77 percent of the companies with direct ownership report the presence of workers on the board. Similarly, 51 percent of the respondents in companies with ESOPs compared to 77 percent in companies with direct ownership indicate that employees influence "important" decisions in the company. In some of the companies, according to our respondents, this influence extends to such decisions as whether or not to make major capital acquisitions.

Employee Ownership and Profitability

Thirty of the companies provided data about profit and we rely on this subset of companies for the analysis of profitability. We employ the ratio

Table 10

Responses to Questions Relevant to Employee Participation in Decisions

	ESOP (N=66-68)	Direct (N=30)	All firms (N=96-98)
Are employees in your company represented by a union?			
Yes	32%	33%	32%
No	68	67	68
Total	100%	100%	100%
Is there employee representation on the Board of Directors of your company?			
Yes	36%	77%	49%
No	64	23	51
Total	100%	100%	100%
Do employees have any direct input into any important decisions besides through a union?			
Yes	51%	77%	56%
No	49	23	44
Total	100%	100%	100%

of pre-tax net profits to sales as a basis for gauging profitability. Furthermore, the ratio for each firm is divided by the ratio in 1976 for the industry as a whole to which the firm belongs.[1] This final ratio is the primary measure of pre-tax profitability of a firm. We made one further adjustment, however, for five firms in our subset: because these firms are directly and wholly owned by employees, the firms follow the practice of distributing a part of their "profit" to employees in the form of wages. This allocation of funds has the effect of depressing the conventional statement of profit, although it has the corresponding advantage of reducing the base upon which tax on profits is computed. The firms justify this adjustment as a cost to the firms of the additional effort and productivity that presumably characterize them.[2] Nonetheless, these monies should be considered part of the profit of the firm for purposes of comparison with the other firms in our set. We therefore took the wage differential between the worker-owners of the firms in question and non-owner-workers (who perform essentially the same jobs as the owners and who receive the union wage rate) as a basis for calculating the amount of money that was diverted from profits to wages. This differential was added to the formally stated profit figure for each of the five firms in question and this final value is taken as the basis for computing the profitability of these firms. While this adjustment seems appropriate as a way of maintaining comparability among firms that employ different accounting procedures, we have also retained, for purpose of analysis, the unadjusted statement of profit. This unadjusted value, we believe, is an overly conservative statement for these firms, but there may be some utility, nonetheless,

---

[1] Robert Morris Associates. Annual statement studies. (1976 ed.) Philadelphia: Credit Division, 1976.

[2] Berman, K. V. Comparative productivity in worker-managed cooperative plywood plants and conventionally run plants. Mimeo, 1976.

in examining profitability defined in this way as well as through the adjusted figure.

The average adjusted profit ratio for the firms in our subset is 1.7; the unadjusted ratio is 1.5. In either case, these values, which are greater than 1.0, indicate that the profitability of the firms in our subset is greater than that of comparable size firms in their respective industries—although we are not able to claim statistical significance for these figures since the variance in profitability among firms is relatively large and the number of cases is small. It is also possible that our "sample" of firms may be select with respect to profitability. We take these figures as suggestive, nonetheless, that employee ownership, in one form or another, may be associated with the profitability of a firm.[1]

Table 11 helps to elaborate this implication. In this table we present the results of a regression analysis in which each of the two indices of profitability (adjusted and unadjusted) is predicted by several aspects of employee ownership. The predictors include:

1. the form of employee ownership, whether direct or through an ESOT (ESOT is scored "0"; direct ownership is scored "1")
2. the percent of employees who participate in the plan
3. the percent of company equity owned by employees (by managers and workers)
4. the percent of company equity owned by the workers themselves
5. whether employees have representatives on the board of directors
6. whether employee stockholders have voting rights.

These predictors jointly explain a substantial amount of the variance in

---

[1] For other studies in which the performance of worker owned plywood firms is compared to that of conventional firms, see Bellas, C., <u>Industrial Democracy and the Worker-Owned Firm</u>. Praeger Publishers: New York, 1972; Berman, K., <u>Worker-Owned Plywood Companies: An Economic Analysis</u>, Pullman, Wash., Washington State University Press, 1967; Comparative productivity in worker-managed cooperative plywood plants and conventionally run plants. Unpublished, 1976. Bernstein, P., <u>Democratization of Organization: Theory, Practice and Further Possibilities</u>, Ph.D. dissertation, Stanford University, 1972. See also Melman, S., Managerial versus cooperative decision making in Israel, <u>Studies in Comparative International Development</u>, 1970-71, 6, 3, who compares the performance of kibbutz firms with conventional firms in Israel.

Table 11

Regression Coefficients for the Predictors of
"Adjusted" and "Unadjusted" Profitability

	Adjusted (N=20)*	Unadjusted (N=25)*
	multiple r=.72	.47
Predictor:		
ESOT (=0) vs. direct ownership (=1)	-.22	-.34
Percent employees participating in plan	-.30	-.31
Percent equity owned internally	-.31	-.19
Percent equity owned by workers	1.02**	.78
Worker representativeness on board of directors	-.18	-.18
Employee stockholders vote	-.05	-.24

*The data necessary to calculate the adjusted profitability ratio are unavailable in five firms of the subset and five firms did not provide information concerning all of the predictors in this regression. The number of cases in the adjusted and unadjusted cells are therefore 20 and 25 respectively.

**$p < .02$

"adjusted" profitability, but only one of the predictors, the amount of equity owned by the workers themselves, proves statistically significant ($p < .02$); the more equity the workers own, the more profitable the firm, other things being equal (beta = 1.02).[1]

The second variable of importance in this analysis, the amount of equity owned internally, has, if anything, a negative relationship with profitability (beta = -.31) but the statistical significance of this variable is marginal, at best, a coefficient of this size occurring about one out of four times by chance. Variation in "internal ownership" in this context is really variation in ownership by <u>managerial personnel</u> since ownership by the workers themselves is controlled in the analysis. The possible implication, therefore, is that increases in the amount of equity owned by managers may have a negative effect <u>if this increase is not accompanied by an increase in the equity owned by the workers</u>. This result is not strong statistically, but it may be worth considering as a hypothesis.

The impact of the remaining variables can easily be attributed to chance but it is nonetheless tantalizing to see that they, too, imply, if anything, negative relationships in the regression. Direct ownership (rather than through an ESOT), the percent of employees who participate in the plan, the existence of worker representatives on the board, and the existence of voting rights show a negative relationship (if anything) to profitability <u>when the percent of equity owned by the workers themselves is controlled</u>.

Prediction of the unadjusted profitability index (second column in Table 11) is not as good as the prediction of the adjusted index, the multiple correlation being only .47, and none of the predictors meet the usual criterion of significance. The pattern of results, however, is

---

[1] "Beta" refers to a standard regression coefficient.

similar to that for the analysis of the adjusted profitability index, and the one predictor that approaches a marginal level of statistical significance in the analysis is the percent of equity owned by the workers (beta = .78, p = .11).

The negative signs associated with several of the variables in Table 11 do not imply (or they would not imply even if they were statistically significant) that these characteristics are associated with low profitability; they imply (or would imply) such a negative association only under the conditions of the regression analysis where, for example, the amount of equity owned by the workers is controlled statistically. In fact, because firms where workers hold a high percent of the equity are likely also to be directly owned, direct ownership, like the amount of worker ownership itself, is positively associated with profitability.

Table 12 helps to illustrate these associations. This table shows the simple, zero order correlations among the variables presented in the regression analysis. Asterisks indicate correlations that are significant at the .05 level or better. We see in this table not only how the predictors may be associated with profitability, but also how the predictors relate to one another. For example, firms in which workers hold a high proportion of the equity tend to be directly owned (r = .68), to have worker representatives on the board (r = .36), and to provide voting rights to employee owners (r = .68). On the other hand, the correlation between the percent of equity owned by the workers and that owned internally (by workers and managers) is not as high as one might expect, in view of the fact that internal ownership includes ownership by workers (r = .34). The proportion of equity owned by managers in many of these firms is relatively large and "internal ownership," therefore, reflects managerial ownership more than worker ownership.

Direct ownership in this table is significantly and positively related to adjusted profitability (r = .48)--unlike the relationship indicated in the regression analysis--because direct ownership is associated with the percent of equity owned by workers, which appears from the regression analysis to be the more basic correlate of profitability. Voting rights is also associated with the percent of equity owned by workers and it, too, shows a positive relationship with adjusted profitability (unlike the relationship in the regression analysis), although the magnitude of the correlation does not meet the criterion of statistical significance, given the small number of cases.

The percent of employees who participate in the ownership plan, however, does _not_ show the relationship to profitability that one might expect from the hypothesis that employee ownership has a positive effect on profitability (r = -.33). The explanation may hinge on the association, or rather lack of association, between the percent of employees who participate and the percent of equity owned by workers (r = .14). Apparently, many firms that have relatively widespread employee ownership in fact involve only a small proportion of the companies' equity in such ownership. Many members, in other words, own very little.

Managers' Estimate of the Effect of Employee Ownership on Productivity and Profit

In an earlier analysis, we found substantial sentiment on the part of managers as well as of workers in favor of the employee ownership plan in a firm that had recently adopted such a plan.[1] According to members of that firm, employee ownership contributed substantially to the satisfaction of all employees as well as to the motivation of workers and ultimately to the productivity and profitability of the company. Records of the firm also indicated that grievances and waste (in the form of expendable tools) declined

---

[1] An employee owned firm. Survey Research Center, Institute for Social Research, The University of Michigan, January 17, 1977.

Table 12

Correlations Among Aspects of Employee Ownership and Profitability

	Profit (Adjusted) (N=20)	Profit (Unadjusted) (N=25)	ESOT vs. Direct Ownership (N=75)	Percent employees participating (N=75)	Percent of equity owned internally (N=75)	Percent of equity owned by workers (N=75)	Workers on board (N=75)
ESOT (=0) vs. Direct Ownership (=1)	.48*	.27					
Percent employees participating	-.33	-.29	-.23*				
Percent of equity owned internally	-.02	-.06	-.10	.25*			
Percent of equity owned by workers	.60*	.31	.68*	.14	.34*		
Workers on board	.24	.08	.36*	.08	.04	.43*	
Employee stockholders vote	.30	.18	.68*	-.11	-.11	.47*	.22*

* $p < .05$

and that productivity and profitability increased during a period immediately following the introduction of the plan (although profitability was higher during one period a number of years earlier).

In the present analysis, a management representative in each firm was asked two questions about the effect of employee ownership on productivity and profit. "Do you think that employee ownership affects profits? Does it increase profits, decrease them, or have no effect?" A similar question was asked concerning productivity. The average response to these questions, 2.6 on a three-point scale, indicates substantial support for employee ownership in the judgement of these managers. Furthermore, the analyses presented in the previous section, which suggest that the employee owned firms are above average in profitability for their respective industries, lend some credence to the claim of these managers. But the managers who are more likely to credit employee ownership for high levels of profit are not necessarily in the more profitable firms of our subset.

Table 13 shows the results of a regression analysis designed to determine which aspects of ownership are associated with the judgement by managers that employee ownership has a positive effect on profit and productivity. Managers in firms in which workers own a high proportion of the equity are no more likely to ascribe positive effects to employee ownership than are managers in firms in which workers own a small proportion of the equity--even though this aspect of employee ownership appears to be the more important correlate of profitability in our analysis (Table 11). On the other hand, employee ownership is more likely to be reported to have positive effects on profit where such ownership is direct, rather than through an ESOT (beta = .46, p = .06) and where workers do not have representatives on the board (beta = -.22 p = .10).

These results do not explain profit and productivity so much as they explain the attitude of managers concerning the possible impact of employee ownership on profit and productivity, and we see in Table 13 some indication (which we shall see repeated below) that the existence of employee representatives on the board may sometimes be associated with negative attitudes on the part of managers. Other things being equal, managers appear to react less positively in firms that have worker representatives on the board than in firms that do not have such representatives.

Employee Ownership and Attitudes of Workers toward Their Job, as Judged by Managers

Each managerial respondent was asked whether employee ownership affected the attitudes of workers toward their job. The average response was .84 on a scale from 0 to 1, where "1" means that work attitudes are better and "0" that they are worse as a result of the ownership plan. The score of .84, therefore, implies that these managers on the average perceive the employee ownership plan to have a substantially positive effect on the attitudes of employees. But as Table 14 suggests, this judgement by managers differs from firm to firm, and it may be less positive where workers have representatives on the board of directors than where they do not. The beta, -.39, which is associated with a provision in the plan for such representation is the only one that proves statistically significant ($p < .01$).

Managers' Satisfaction with the Employee Ownership Plan

The managerial respondent in each firm was asked, "Are you satisfied with the way employee ownership is working?" The average response to this question is 2.8, which implies in general a high degree of satisfaction--"3" being the highest possible score. Table 15 shows how aspects of employee ownership are associated with this satisfaction.

Table 13

Regression Coefficients for the Predictors of
Manager's Estimate of the Effect of Employee
Ownership on Productivity and Profit
(N=71)

multiple r=.35

Predictor:

ESOT (=0) vs. direct ownership (=1)	.46**
Percent employees participating in plan	.12
Percent equity owned by employees	-.12
Percent equity owned by workers	-.06
Worker representatives on the board (no=0; yes=1)	-.22*
Employee owners vote (no=0; yes=1)	-.07

**p=.06

*p=.10

Table 14

Regression Coefficients for the Predictors of Worker's
Attitudes Toward Their Job, as Judged by Managers
(N=70)

multiple r=.44

Predictor:

ESOT (=0) vs. direct ownership (=1)	.35
Percent employees participating in plan	.15
Percent equity owned by employees	-.13
Percent equity owned by workers	-.05
Worker representatives on the board (no=0; yes=1)	-.39*
Employee owners vote (no=0; yes=1)	.08

---

*p=.004

Table 15

Regression Coefficients for the Predictors of Manager's
Satisfaction with the Employee Ownership Plan
(N=70)

multiple r=.42

Predictor:

ESOT (=0) vs. direct ownership (=1)	.69*
Percent employees participating in plan	.28**
Percent equity owned by employees	.17
Percent equity owned by workers	-.24
Worker representatives on the board (no=0; yes=1)	-.12
Employee owners vote (no=0; yes=1)	-.22

---

*$p < .004$

**$p < .05$

Two variables prove significant in this regression. Managers are more satisfied with the plan where ownership is direct rather than through an ESOT (beta = .69, p < .004) and where the percent of employees who participate in the plan is relatively large (beta = .28, p < .05). It seems reasonable that managers should think well of the plan where participation is widespread. On the other hand, we have seen that widespread ownership is not associated with profitability; such ownership may very well mean that many employees own only a very small fraction of the equity--and it is the amount of equity owned by workers that appears to be the most important correlate of profitability.

Employee Ownership and Employee Influence

Each managerial respondent was asked, "Do employees have any direct input into any important decisions besides through a union?" Simple, zero order correlations indicate that managers judge worker influence to be relatively high in firms where the percent of equity owned by workers is relatively great ($r = .42^*$), ownership is direct ($r = .25^*$), employees have representatives on the board ($r = .25^*$), and employee-owners have voting rights ($r = .22^*$). One of these variables, the percent of equity owned by workers is the relatively more important one in a regression analysis, as can be seen in Table 16.

Table 17 provides the simple, zero order correlations between managers' satisfaction with the plan and their estimates of (1) the influence that workers have, (2) the plan's effect on productivity and profit, and (3) the

---
* p < .05.

Table 16

Regression Coefficients for the Predictors of
Employee Influence, as Judged by Managers
(N=68)

multiple r=.50

Predictor:

ESOT (=0) vs. direct ownership (=1)	-.08
Percent employees participating in plan	-.05
Percent equity owned by employees	-.03
Percent equity owned by workers	.44*
Worker representatives on the board (no=0; yes=1)	.12
Employee owners vote (no=0; yes=1)	.09

---

* p=.04

plan's effect on workers' job attitudes. All of these variables, with the exception of the one concerning worker influence, relate positively to one another, again indicating that while managers tend to be consistent in appraising the implications of employee ownership, they do not include worker influence as part of their positive conception of such ownership.

Conclusions

Some degree of employee ownership of firms is not uncommon in this country, although examples in which non-managerial employees own a substantial part of the equity of the company are rare. Nonetheless, data about such companies offer preliminary evidence concerning the possible impact of expanded ownership on the economic viability of firms and on their ability to save jobs. We are led on the basis of these data to the following tentative conclusions.

First, the industrial relations climate in employee owned firms appears to be good, in the judgement of managerial respondents. Second, managerial respondents in these firms see employee ownership as having a positive effect on productivity and profit in the firm. Third, the employee owned firms that we have studied do appear to be profitable--perhaps more profitable than comparable, conventionally owned firms. Fourth, the single most important correlate of profitability among the aspects of ownership that we have studied is the percent of the company's equity owned by the workers themselves. Fifth, while the influence that workers have in the firm, as judged by managers, is a function of the amount of equity that the workers own, managers' evaluation of the ownership plan is not affected in a positive way by either the amount of ownership held by the workers or the amount of influence exercised by the workers. Managers appear to be more favorably disposed toward the plan where participation in ownership is widespread among

Table 17

Correlations Among Responses of Managers
Concerning Aspects of Employee Ownership
(N=90)

	Managers satisfied with plan	Positive effect on profit and productivity	Employees have influence
Positive effect on workers attitudes	.45*	.54*	.11
Managers satisfied with plan		.34*	.01
Positive effect on profit and productivity			-.07

*$p < .01$

employees, even though widespread participation may involve only a small fraction of the company's equity.

Several of the firms we studied adopted their ownership plan specifically as a way of saving the plant from economic collapse and saving the jobs in the plant. Some adopted the ownership plan for other financial reasons or for moral reasons. But in either case, the data of this report, indicate that employee ownership may contribute to the economic viability of a firm and to the economic well being of members as well as to the quality of working life within the firm.

The data suggest that the impact of employee ownership on unemployment in specific firms might be viewed from the point of view of prevention as well as from the point of view of cure. In the latter case, a firm in which the threat of unemployment is imminent might be bought by employees as a way of saving their jobs. We have examples in our data of this form of "cure." On the other hand, a healthy firm might move into employee ownership as a way of strengthening its performance so that the loss of jobs will not be threatened in the first place. Our data also include firms of this type.

We offer the above conclusions as tentative. The firms for which we have measures of profit may be select and our analyses are based on correlations that illustrate association among variables; they do not prove causation. The results of these analyses, however, are sufficiently encouraging to justify a detailed longitudinal (historical) study of a number of firms over a period of years. Such a study should include measures of the attitudes and motivations of all employees within the firms as well as measures of the performance of the firms.

II. An Employee Owned Firm[1]

This section concerns one firm that was acquired by its employees through an employee stock owners trust. The company was acquired by its employees following a decision by the original owner to liquidate because of a poor profitability picture. The plant's closing would have meant the loss of jobs for its 500 employees as well as for an estimated 100 to 200 others whose jobs depended indirectly on the plant. Several of the company's officers, with the backing of the employees arranged to borrow $10,000,000 to purchase the company and to keep it in operation. Half of the borrowed sum came from a revolving account established in the community by the Economic Development Administration as a means of helping to provide employment in the community. The remaining portion was borrowed from other, conventional sources.

Summary

The data that we report in this section were collected approximately 18 months after the acquisition and they came from two sources. First, are data concerning the attitudes and perceptions of company personnel obtained through interviews with 51 randomly selected persons in the company. Second, are data from company records that provide information about profit, worker productivity, absences, grievances, injuries, and other indicators of company performance.

---

[1] This section was prepared by Michael Conte, Fred Leech, Donna McCulloch, and Arnold Tannenbaum. We thank R. J. Bullock for his help in planning the analysis of the financial data provided by the company. We also very much appreciate the substantial help provided by the officers and employees of the company in making this report possible.

The data from these diverse sources are in large measure consistent in their implication that performance has improved at the company in recent years and that the level of morale and worker motivation has increased since the change in ownership. The causes of improvement can not be determined with certainty from the preliminary analysis presented here, although the reports of many company personnel, including workers and managers indicate that at least some of the improvement is attributable to the change in ownership and to the employee stock ownership plan. We hope to be able to answer the question of causality with more certainty as additional data become available to us and as more detailed analyses are undertaken.

Employee Attitudes and Perceptions

Changes in the company since the Employee Stock Ownership Plan

Practically all the workers and managers whom we interviewed indicated that the company had changed for the better since the employee stock ownership plan was introduced. (See Table 1.) Improvements in the company described by the respondents fell primarily into several categories (See Table 2.) First, about half of the workers and managers mentioned that the relationships between people had improved and that people worked better together now that they all owned the company. For instance, one worker stated that:

> You have everyone more united...and you have a better outlook on coming to work. It seems as if you're working for yourself. You just don't come in and put in your eight hours. It's kind of a psychological thing. You work like any other job but it's a psychological thing where you are working for yourself like you're in business for yourself.

Another remarked that, "I feel it's more of a family now, more homey. It's a pleasure to work here." One manager put it this way:

> I think we're a closer knit family. There's more feeling of ownership among the employees. Naturally, we still have a few employees we still have got to get that word to, that final convincing that they are owners. Over all, it's been a very healthy change.

Another manager pointed out that a problem that might have been considered a management problem, "Now it's everyone's problem."

Second, nearly three-quarters of the managers and close to half of the workers felt that morale had improved and that people were more conscientious about their jobs. For example, one manager stated that, "I think the morale is a lot better than it was before--you've got more of a feeling of personal pride among the workers," and another claimed "the interest of the employees

Table 1

Question: Have things changed at the company since the employee stock ownership plan has been introduced... are they better, worse, or about the same as before?

	% Workers (N=40)	% Managers (N=11)	% Total (N=51)
Better	93	82	90
Better in some ways	2	9	4
Worse	0	0	0
No different	5	9	6
	100%	100%	100%

Table 2

Question: In what ways have things changed?

	% Workers* (N=40)	% Managers* (N=11)	% Total* (N=51)
More of a united effort; more of a family; it's our company; better relations and cooperation between people and departments; better communications; more shared responsibility	58	45	55
Better attitudes and morale; more interest in work and company affairs; more conscientious; better effort	45	73	51
Better benefits; more bonuses; more pay; improved working conditions; more vacation; holiday turkey	48	27	43
Less waste; less absenteeism	10	18	12
More promising future; more confidence in the future; business is picking up; orders are better; fewer layoffs; in future we should be able to catch up to other plants in wages	13	9	12
Some workers still suspicious; poor communications in some cases	3	9	4
We have more of a voice in the company; participating more	8	0	6

*Percentages need not add to 100 because of multiple responses.

is more noteworthy. Everyone is trying a little harder." One worker felt that:

> The guys are more conscientious about their work. They feel they got to put out a much better product now because that's what's going to make more business for us. They do a little better work now than they did before.

A third category of comments, noted somewhat more by the workers than by the managers, concerns benefits and working conditions. For example, one worker was pleased with the new benefits even though he felt that working conditions had not changed appreciably.

> Yes, now workwise it's about the same in our department, but in benefits it's changed a lot. Really good, really good. I've never had it so good. We get raises more often and bonuses; week's pay; we get turkeys at Thanksgiving and things like that we never had before.

Another worker stated,

> Well, I think it has changed drastically because with [the former owner], we weren't getting what we're getting now. It's a different ballgame now. It's our company and they're treating us good. They give us bonuses; they give us extra checks, you know like vacation. They give us a couple of weeks vacation added in. [The former owner] never did that to us. They took all the money and they claimed they weren't making a profit. So far as the employee-owned is, in my opinion, I like it.

Reduction in waste and absenteeism were mentioned specifically by a number of respondents. For example, one worker said,

> Everybody is not so willing to throw a part away anymore which was one of the first signs they cared about the compnay. Scrap is held to a minimum. A ten minute break is now a 15 minute break where it used to be a half hour or 45 minute break. They're a little more conscious of a lot of small things.

Another person proclaimed, "My particular job is taking care of the scrap and since this last year I noticed the scrap off the machines I picked up as a lesser amount than previously."

A fifth category concerns the future of the company, which according to several workers and managers looks promising. As one worker put it,

"There's much more confidence in the future. This is one of main things we have today that we didn't have before."

Finally, a small number of respondents mentioned that employees had more of a voice in the company, and a few indicated that some workers were still suspicious or that communications were not good. Negative comments of this kind were rare.

Attitude of Management Toward Employees

Managers and workers were asked about the attitude of management toward employees. Nearly three-quarters of the managers interviewed and about half of the workers felt that the attitude of management had changed for the better. About one-fifth of the managers and nearly half of the workers felt that no change had occurred, and small percentages of both groups felt that managerial attitudes were better in some ways but worse in others. None of the respondents felt that attitudes were worse. (Table 3.)

Change in the attitudes of management reported by respondents fall into several categories (Table 4). A fairly high proportion of both groups (64 percent of the managers and 43 percent of the workers) felt that workers were treated better by managers and more like owners and that communication was better. Thus, one worker felt that management was more considerate of him and described some of the consequences of this:

> They listen to our problems more readily. The people on the floor have to work with certain problems all day, week in and week out, year in and year out, and management is beginning to realize that and starting to listen to us where they didn't before, and it's good employee-employer relationships because if you know someone will listen to your problems, you feel more like a human and when you take the dehumanization out of the job, there's more productivity, you're more responsible, you're more willing to work more overtime, and less tension, and it's a pretty good deal all around.

Table 3

Question: Has the attitude of managers toward employees changed...
for better or for worse?

	% Workers (N=40)	% Managers (N=11)	% Total (N=51)
Better	53	73	57
Better in some ways, worse in others	2	9	4
Worse	0	0	0
No different	45	18	39
	100%	100%	100%

Table 4

Question: In what way has attitude of managers toward employees changed?

	% Workers* (N=40)	% Managers* (N=11)	% Total* (N=51)
Better communications; workers treated as owners; more consideration; we work better together; more cooperation	43	64	47
Workers have more of a voice in decision-making; management doesn't give "orders" anymore; management goes to workers for ideas	3	36	10
Management has given worker better benefits, working conditions, and equipment	10	0	8
No change: we've always gotten along; it was always good and still is	8	9	8
No change: management has not improved in attitudes toward workers; management is management and workers are workers; the hierarchy is still the same	8	9	8
Management is tighter/stricter around the shop	3	0	2
Workers can be too assertive	0	9	2

* See footnote Table 2

Another worker felt that communications were better in that workers were better informed of managerial actions:

> We're more informed now on management's side of the company. They are telling us what's going on inside the company, what they have planned and how things are going.

One manager stated,

> I used to be a supervisor out in the shop and I think after the change took place we looked at the union guys as more of an equal rather than a subordinate that just did what we wanted him to.

About one-third of the managers and a small percentage of the workers felt that managers have given workers a greater say in decision-making and that they do not give "orders" to workers anymore. One manager commented that workers have "a little bit more responsibility in the decision-making process," and another stated that,

> We now look at him as a source of improvements. We go to them for ideas on how to improve things. Before we did it our way and that was it, but now we ask for ideas. I think it's more of an equal basis now.

One foreman described his alternative procedure to giving "orders" when he needed something done:

> Because as a foreman, at one time, we used to tell them what to do. Now, after all you're dealing with an owner. So we use a different approach. I say well, what do you want your foremen to do?... I say do you want me to enforce this or don't you. And 90, oh just about 100, percent of the time they say yes, we want this enforced, even if it applies to them. So, it kind of turned us around a little bit, but it works out good.

A small group of workers (10 percent) mentioned that management had given them more benefits. As has been shown, however, not all of the respondents felt that management's attitudes had changed. Many respondents did not elaborate on why they felt there was no change. However, of those who did, two distinct groups emerged. One group felt that relations were always fairly good between managers and workers and that nothing had changed in this respect. A typical comment of this sort by a worker was, "It's hard to say because they've always been nice and cared about the employees...." The other group made comments suggesting that the old hierarchy was still there and that management was management and labor was labor. One worker expressed his dismay with this, stating:

> No, I don't believe so, it's still the same. That's one thing that disappoints me. Because there seems to be still that dividing line where I don't think it should be. Well, it should be to an extent, but not the same as it was. Well, like they're still working for the conglomerate, and we're still more or less union.

On the negative side, one manager suggested that workers were getting too assertive and one worker complained that managers were stricter around the shop and wouldn't give him everything he wanted anymore.

Attitude of Employees toward Management

Respondents were invited to comment about changes in the attitude of employees toward management. A majority of both groups felt that employee attitudes had improved. (Table 5.)

Table 6 provides a categorization of the changes indicated by respondents. 45 percent of workers and managers felt that working relationships between the two groups were improved in that better communication, more confidence and respect for managers and improved teamwork prevailed. One worker stated:

> The attitude of employees toward management now is not so negative, not so resentful of the authority they have. They figure whatever they're doing is for our success as a whole rather than money in the pockets of the higher-ups.

Another worker commented, "They think we're more human, at least to do the right thing...we feel like we're partners now and want to keep it that way." One manager saw a change in employee attitudes in this way:

> Morally speaking or philosophically, they realize that we can all see we're working together and the distinction between the two--

Table 5

Question: Has the attitude of employees toward management changed...for better or for worse?

	% Workers (N=40)	% Managers (N=11)	% Total (N=51)
Better	58	55	57
Better in some ways, worse in others	5	0	4
Worse	2	18	6
No different	35	27	33
	100%	100%	100%

Table 6

Question: In what ways has the attitude of employees toward management changed?

	% Workers* (N=40)	% Managers* (N=11)	% Total* (N=51)
We work better together, more of a team; better communication; better, friendlier relations; more confidence and respect; better cooperation	45	45	45
Workers take on increased responsibility; they try to solve things before they go to managers; management is more conscientious; trying harder	8	18	10
Workers have more say in decisions; workers can get results from their decisions	5	9	6
No layoffs	3	0	2
Some workers are still suspicious of management; fear that management is getting a bigger cut of the shares; management is still management and workers are still workers	10	27	14
Miscellaneous	15	27	18

*See Footnote Table 2

> i.e., 'they're the bad guys and we're the good guys'--that's been changing.

Another manager stated:

> We seem like we're working more as a team, where before it was always union and management, now it's almost like all owners. It's all teamwork, and I notice that people go over and help each other now where in the old days they used to say, 'hey, find somebody to help that guy.' Now, a man has a problem, three or four fellows come over and help him.

Another group of respondents (18 percent of the managers and 8 percent of the workers) felt that workers were taking on increased responsibilities or that management was more conscientious. One manager proclaimed that, "They're willing to accept some of our problems, and they're trying to help solve these problems before they even come to us." A worker remarked, "Oh yeah. They're trying to make the product better so they can sell it. Before it was like [the conglomerate] was in charge."

Some of those who felt that employees' attitudes toward management had remained the same or worsened expressed the opinion that workers were suspicious of management or that workers felt that management would come out with most of the shares. One manager elaborated upon this problem, stating:

> ...there is the suspicion of empire building. The prime thing is the way the shares are being divided by salary and they have the idea that the higher positions and management will come out with the majority of the shares. We've proved that management will come out with 33 percent and that the union will come out with 66 percent, but it's very difficult to convince these guys and they're still very suspicious. But I think this will change--you will change them when they receive two or three bonuses, etc., i.e., something they've never had before.

A worker confirmed this manager's opinion, stating,

> Well, some of them think that management gets a little better deal out of ESOP than they are. They're thinking moneywise to theirself. They figure that because management makes better wages, they're gonna get a big cut out of the share, I guess.

Other causes for suspicion included the union problem and the fact that many workers lost their pension when the ownership changed from conglomerate to workers. This was especially problematic for some senior employees who had accumulated substantial equity in the pension plan under the former owners, but who did not have quite enough seniority to claim their pension rights at the time of the transfer of ownership—but they would have lost those rights in any case had the company been liquidated.

One worker described some of these problems:

> It's still a little bit suspicious. They don't know how far management will go. We still have a union problem here and we don't know how it will go. These older persons who lost out on the pension are in bad shape. We don't know how that is going to go.

Attitude of Employees toward Their Work

When asked whether employees' attitudes toward their work had changed most respondents, workers and managers alike, reported an improvement. (Table 7.) A high percentage of both groups (36 percent of the managers and 50 percent of the workers) mentioned that workers were more interested in their jobs because they felt they were working for themselves or that company success was a result of their efforts (Table 8). Thus, one manager claimed, "They feel a little bit more responsibility for quality workmanship, being it is their own company." Another manager described how reward depends on performance, stating:

> We know what we sell it [the product] for, and we can say, 'okay, fellows, every time one of those go out it's $8000 profit,' and you're back to dollars again and you're talking language they can understand and by doing this, you can get a little more enthusiasm out of the guys.

Some of the workers made similar comments. Regarding the feeling of ownership, one stated, "I seem to think I want to get it out better than I did because I know it's for me." And another remarked,

> I think we're getting a little better work out of people now. Now we got something to work for. Before we were working for a company. Now we're working for ourselves.

In the same fashion, another claimed,

> Well, now everybody is more or less in making money for themselves. It's their work, not just the company's. Before the money was going into somebody else's pocket. Now it's our own.

Table 7

Question: Has the attitude of employees toward their work changed...for better or for worse?

	% Workers (N=40)	% Managers (N=11)	% Total (N=51)
Better	83	91	84
Better in some ways, worse in others	0	0	0
Worse	2	0	2
No difference	13	9	12
Not ascertained	2	0	2
	100%	100%	100%

Table 8

Question: In what ways has the attitude of employees toward their work changed?

	% Workers* (N=40)	% Managers* (N=11)	% Total* (N-51)
Workers feel that they are working for themselves; realize that their salary is contingent upon their performance; workers have more interest in their jobs; company success is a result of their effort; better atmosphere	50	36	47
More conscientious; trying harder; putting more time in; not as much goofing off; less absenteeism	35	27	33
More precision; better quality of work; less waste	25	36	27
Worker making more money; getting ahead better	8	0	6
Greater quantity of work; higher productivity	3	9	4
More teamwork; workers help each other more	0	9	2

* See footnote Table 2

About a quarter of the managers and a third of the workers mentioned that employees were more conscientious and were putting in a greater effort. One manager stated that "They're more conscientious in what they do and how they perform." The workers expressed much the same opinion with one stating, "There isn't as much goofing off as there used to be" and another commenting,

> As far as I can see, I'd say I know my attitude has changed. I feel more conscientious about my job and I want to do my job to the best of my ability. I can't really speak for a whole lot of other people but the ones I talk to seem to be more conscientious about their jobs. I'd say yes, their attitudes have changed for the better.

About one-third of the managers and one-fourth of the workers felt that this extra effort was paying off in terms of better quality of work and decreased waste. One manager replied,

> The large percentage of the employees are more cost conscious, more scrap conscious, and are trying harder not to run scrap and still maintain a high level of earnings.

One worker put it bluntly, stating, "We're a little more careful about what we do and how much [we] waste. It's our money now." And another made a similar remark, "They're trying to put out good parts. If we don't run good parts, it's going to hurt us, come right out of our pocket." A third stated,

> They're doing a better job all around now. Like piece work jobs--they're not rushing right through because they don't want to get it back.

Smaller numbers of managers and workers mentioned other changes in the attitudes of employees toward their work. Some felt that "their production was on the better side." Others thought that there was more of a team spirit and that workers were helping each other out more. Thus one manager commented:

> They're working more as a team now...If a guy's got a problem, everybody used to sit back, and say 'I'm glad it's not me.' Now they feel just the other way around. It's us now.

Some workers felt that employee attitudes toward work had improved because the employees were making more money and getting ahead better.

Change in the Way Decisions are Made

While the employee stock ownership plan had strong effects on the attitudes of the respondents, it appears that the decision-making structure has not changed very much, according to most respondents. When respondents were asked whether there had been any change in the way decisions that affected them were made, a majority felt that there had been no change. (Table 9.)

Eighteen percent of the respondents, however, felt that they had more say, and that they were consulted about major decisions, that they were not given orders, or that formal channels, such as representation on the board of directors or employee votes, provided a means of participation in decision-making. One supervisor expresses this sentiment well, stating,

> As far as major decisions, I think we have more of a say as far as suggesting what might be done. We're allowed to put in our suggestions and they're heard, and management, upper management, is not afraid to listen to us, and they're willing to sit down and listen to an idea if we've got one. I know that if we go back and say this is the way it should be done, well, they come back and say, 'Well, you show us how it should be done.' It's a lot different than it was before. I think before, upper management just did it and that was it and I've been in all the way from the union up to management and I think it's changed. I think we have more of a say.

A worker felt there was a change in his foreman's order-giving behavior:

> I'm working as a fork lifter now. Instead of telling the guys, they ask the guys, they ask the guys in a sort of round about way that they're not forcing the person to do something and I feel it helps us in better relations between the management or even the foreman and the driver. I'll be walking around and one of the foreman may ask me to do something and he'll say when you get time and I'll say I got time now. I'll do it. I got that attitude. I like to do it. It's good.

Table 9

Question: Has there been any change in the way decisions that affect you are made?

	% Workers* (N=40)	% Managers* (N=11)	% Total* (N=51)
No change	68	55	65
We have more say; they ask for our opinion before making major decisions; they listen to us more; more equality; they don't give orders; we have representatives on the board of directors; they take employee votes	18	18	18
Attitudes of management better; they are for the worker	10	0	8
Decisions made by local personnel, not conglomerate	0	9	2
We may have more say in the future; will have more say when we own more stock; drastic changes take time	5	9	6
Decisions that were made by me are now made higher up; management used to set the pay scale, now the board does it	0	18	4
Workers have less say now, before we had a union even if it was weak	3	0	2

* See footnote Table 2

Another worker concentrated on the more formal aspects, stating:

> Now, if we've got something major, more or less, they come to us and get our opinion first and see how the guys feel about it around here. Some things they don't ask us, but most of the major stuff they ask us first. Well, they ask us like if we wanted to change the incentive program around a little bit on piece work and they sent out pamphlets and explained everything and asked our opinion of it and we could either vote yes or no or leave some other kind of answer. It was left up to us what we wanted to do with it.

A small number of managers and workers felt that although there were no changes now, they would have more say in the future, especially when they owned more stock and had some experience with participation. In this fashion, one manager stated,

> Again, I think it will be a certain period of time. They want to make certain changes but you have to learn to walk before you can run. This is the wisest move. This is what the Board of Directors is trying to do.

One of the workers gave his viewpoint, stating,

> Well, I don't think there is [a change] yet. There supposedly is supposed to be within the next three years I think it is. Well, they might listen to certain ones more now than they did about ideas and ways of doing things better. But in time, it's supposed to be to the point where we all have a say-so, if we have an improvement to make or something.

Another worker explained this in terms of percentage of stock owned:

> I'm looking at it from long range. Right now we really don't have any input, and say, because at this point, I feel we have a small percentage of the stock. Until we are in 100 percent of control then we will have more input and can have more control.

A small number of managers indicated that they had more say because decisions were currently made by local personnel rather than by the conglomerate. Others, however, felt that decisions were made at a higher level than before and that some of the decisions that were previously made by them were made higher up. One such manager commented, "Well, now in our pay scale and like that, where it used to be a management problem, now the board settles it."

A small number of workers remarked that they might have more say now than before because the attitude of their managers was better and that they were for the workers. Others stated that workers have less say now because they no longer have their union. One of these workers stated,

> No, they're still made the same; management makes them. Sometimes I think we got less say now. Well, before they had a union, but we didn't feel we was getting much out of it but we could hide behind them, for all the good it did...There would be like one or two guys from the union, which maybe tended to go the other way from the worker's point of view, would try to help, see what they could get out of it, which wasn't usually too much. But now since we just about don't have one, it's not that much to hide behind, so that they just take over.

General Opinions of the Stock Ownership Plan

When asked how they felt about the stock ownership plan, most respondents reacted favorably. Many of them commented specifically upon the benefits they had received and the feeling of togetherness and ownership it had created and expressed a favorable outlook for the future. Of the small group who gave negative or mixed answers, some complained that the money was divided up unfairly, that they did not have the influence that they should have or that they lost their pension in the change of ownership.

Again the answers of managers and workers were similar to one another. (Table 10.) Respondents (82 percent of the managers and 77 percent of the workers) made positive statements about employee stock ownership. As far as specific remarks are concerned nearly three-quarters of the managers and one-third of the workers drew attention to the improved benefits and working conditions that accompanied the plan. As one worker put it,

> It feels okay. We do get bonuses we didn't get before. I worked for 27 years and never even got a turkey at Thanksgiving. Now we get bonuses and vacations, we never got those things before. It's okay now. I like it.

Table 10

Question: How do you feel about the stock ownership plan?

	% Workers (N=40)	% Managers (N=11)	% Total (N=51)
General tone of comments			
Positive - I like it, a good idea, an improvement, things are better	77	82	78
Mixed - I like some things about it but not others; better in some ways, worse in others	10	0	8
Negative - I don't like it, it doesn't really give you influence, unfair, things are worse	13 / 100%	18 / 100%	14 / 100%

	% Workers*	% Managers*	% Total*
Specific remarks			
Better benefits; better retirement provision; bonuses; better pension; more vacation; holiday turkey; improved working conditions; shares divided up fairly	35	73	43
We're all working together; it's good to be a part of something; working for yourself, you work harder and care about what goes on; better relations; better atmosphere	23	45	27
It has real possibilities; it will get even better in the future; they will improve it; will be more of a feeling of ownership in the future when employees get more stock	20	36	24
I have a job now because of it; it's worth it to stay with the company rather than to get another job	10	9	10
Financial gains for the company	3	9	4
Contingent answers: depends on business and outlook; if everyone is behind it, it will work; if problems get worked out, will be good; if it stays solven as long as we make money	15	0	12
I lost my pension in the change over; lost my seniority	10	9	10
Stock ownership does not necessarily give one influence; workers don't feel they have influence.	0	18	4
Don't like the way the stock is divided/money handled; shouldn't have to put $1000 in; stocks should be equally shared - not based on your salary; shouldn't have to wait 10 years to take money out	13	0	10

*See footnote Table 2

Another worker commented,

> I like it. In the first year what I've gained it took me 21 years on the previous pension plan and I contributed to that and look what I got in one year plus all the other benefits--bonuses two years in a row, turkey for Christmas, an extra week for vacation and an extra week at Christmas.

A manager felt that the pension plan provided was superior to ones he had previously encountered:

> If it works out like it's supposed to, I think it's a pretty good deal. It gives a guy, where normally he has to work 30 years to draw a pension, he can now work ten or 15 years and [if he] left, he would at least still get something.

Another fairly large group of respondents (45 percent of the managers and 23 percent of the workers) made remarks about the change in atmosphere at the company, and how the feeling of ownership created a spirit of togetherness and a desire to work harder. Thus, one worker commented,

> I think stock ownership makes a person want to do the best he can because it's for his own good. When you're treated right, you want to do right.

In a similar fashion, another worker commented,

> I feel as though it's something new when I come through the door. It's something I do for me. Everyone else is working for me too. We, as employees, were so fortunate to have a man like [the president.] He worked real hard and seemed to care about us all here.

One of the managers gave a somewhat more elaborate description of the effects of the feeling of ownership:

> Let's assume that somebody locally just bought us out. I don't think that the morale would be as high as it is now. I would still be of that opinion, that I'm working for somebody else, [that] I'm not working for myself...[but] right now you're working for yourself really. With ESOP, for instance, if I were working for [another company], down the street here, they had bought us, we really wouldn't be worried too much about how much we spent for this and how much overtime we put in here, but now being ESOP you start looking at your watch and say, 'gee, I'm working too much overtime and that's taken out of my over-all, that's taken off the top of the cream there and I don't like that.' So you have a little more pride and you're a little more conscious of what happens whereas if somebody else owns you, you're just not conscious of it. You just don't have that feeling. It's their money.

Other respondents (36 percent of the managers and 20 percent of the workers) focused upon the favorable outlook for the future and expressed their conviction that the plan will be improved even more. One worker briefly stated, "I'm in favor of it. In the long run it will pay off for us. Say ten years from now. So far we've been doing pretty good." Similarly, one manager remarked, "I think it will snowball as it improves and it will improve more." And another stated:

> After three years when employees actually have in their possession shares of stock that they know is their's and a percentage of it that even if they leave the company and they can figure out what that percentage will be, that's when your real feeling of ownership will be there. I'm certainly hoping for it.

Smaller numbers of managers and workers cited the fact that they still had jobs (9 percent of managers and 10 percent of workers) or that the company was making financial gains (9 percent of the managers and 3 percent of workers) as evidence of the plan's success. As one worker commented:

> I'm very glad we got it or otherwise we'd be out of a job. I don't know how it will affect us in the future or anything like that, but we do have jobs. Otherwise we wouldn't have jobs. We'd be looking for jobs.

In addition, a number of workers (15 percent) gave contingent answers, i.e., they would like the plan if it succeeded and if certain conditions are met. As one commented,

> I think it's a good idea. If everybody gets together on this thing and puts 100 percent into it, it's all going to come back on us. It will work out for us people, if it works out, but it's got to be a 100 percent deal, You can't have 80 percent for it and 20 percent not.

On the negative side, some respondents commented on their hard feelings over losing their pensions or that they were not as influential as they felt they should be or that they felt that the money was unfairly divided.

A small percentage of both workers and managers expressed bitterness over the loss of their pensions when ownership changed hands. One worker stated,

> Of course the only thing I can complain about is the pension. I got 25 years and no pension. They tell me I'm too young to get a pension. I can't go back 25 years and start again...

A manager echoed this statement:

> I lost my pension on the old plan and I'd like to see it work because it means a lot to me. I was here 22 years. I know it's a selfish reason but everybody's in the same way.

Some managers and supervisory personnel (18 percent) pointed out that stock ownership and increased influence do not necessarily go hand-in-hand. As one stated,

> Stock ownership does not really give stock owners influence in the company. Today it's a one man corporation--the president. He appoints the board of directors. The board of directors appoints the employee trust committee. It's one continuous circle. After 15-18 years when voting rights are vested, the shareholders will have appreciable influence. I am a bit skeptical of the ability of management to change. The Bank will not make management change. This is not a criticism of ESOP; it's a comment about the company.

Some workers (13 percent) were critical of the actual financial operation of the plan and felt that management and certain types of workers were getting a disproportionate number of shares. One worker had a number of complaints:

> I don't like the way it's set up. You got to put $1000 in before you're eligible to participate, plus stock shares are based on the amount of money you make, which I don't think is a fair way of doing it. I'd rather see it set up for amount of hours at work rather than amount of money--i.e., it should be an equal sharing. If you are a lower paid day worker rather than a piece worker, it's not fair. You got the same amount of responsibility. It takes everybody to do a job. I don't think it's a fair way of doing it. Also, at the age of 65, you can't call it profit sharing. All it amounts to is a retirement plan at 65. You retire or don't live to see it. It should be after 10 years, it should be 100 percent vested and you should be able to take that money out. After all, it is your money.

This worker may be revealing a misunderstanding of one aspect of the plan when he states that $1000 is required for eligibility. According to company officers, the plan prohibits that persons can "buy into" the plan. Another worker also complained about the way the stock is distributed, but he acknowledged that he did not really understand the plan:

> I feel all right about it, if we could make sense out of it. The way they spell it out, we don't know how much money we got, how much stock we got, or what they do with our stock after they have got it, which I suppose they do send us some machinery and different things, but how that works don't make too much sense to me. They don't spell it out clearly like an ordinary person could make sense of it. To them it probably does. To us it don't make sense. Unless we take it to a lawyer and have him figure it out and they cost you money. Well, I'm dissatisfied in a few ways. Like they said there's 12 people gets two-thirds of it. Well, that is wrong, because they're getting the highest wages to begin with. I still say, whatever profit come in through the back door should be split equally among the men plus the supervision. Not that they get a bigger share than the rest of us, and not to go by wages because wages vary, fluctuate quite a bit. Now, like me, I'm mostly on day work. All right, I'd be the one that would collect the smallest amount and I put out the same production as the other guys. That's where it hurts the smaller man with smaller wages. Where you're on piece work you can make your $60 a day and that's what they go by, the average of it. So where I make maybe $35, $40 a day, so I'm losing money.

This reaction may illustrate how some misunderstanding can arise when complex information is communicated to a large number of persons. It may also illustrate a real difference in point of view between at least some persons within the plant.

Company Performance

The morale and motivation of company personnel has improved as a result of the ownership plan, according to employees. According to these persons, employees are working more efficiently and more carefully because of the plan and they are contributing in this way to the success of the company. In fact, a number of measures of company performance based on company records do indicate improvement in recent years, although we are not able to determine from the available data how much of the improvement is attributable to the ESOP itself. The purchase of the company by employees was attended by other significant changes, including the establishment of an independent corporate identity, and some turnover in high level personnel. Each of these changes may have had an effect on corporate performance, quite apart from the ESOP itself. For example, according to some company officers, decision making has been facilitated and made more effective because decisions that had heretofore been centralized at conglomerate headquarters are now made within the plant itself. Furthermore, a number of significant changes in company strategy regarding marketing, production, and accounting were introduced along with the change in ownership. These strategies and some of their implications include:

- reduction in the backlog of orders which the company was having difficulty meeting efficiently and the elimination in that backlog of under-priced items
- stabilization of monthly sales
- decrease in the average collection time for accounts receivable
- reduction in annual insurance premiums (for the same degree of coverage)
- purchase of a small new division

Profit is one index of company performance. The years 1970 through 1975 were periods of loss for the company. The earlier years in this period, however, were difficult for the industry as a whole. Domestic new orders fell drastically in 1969 and did not rise to their previous level until the early part of 1973. The company did not do much worse than average for its class in 1972. In 1973, however, the industry in general returned to previous levels of profitability, while the company did not. The company did not move into the black until after the employee takeover. Monthly profit (net income before taxes) since that time has been consistently positive and the flow of profits has been stable.

The productivity of workers on jobs that have time standards appears also to have increased since the change in ownership and this increase in the <u>amount</u> of work turned out by each employee has not occurred at the expense of the <u>quality</u> of that work as measured by the rate of returns of the product from customers. The rate of these returns has gone down compared to the pre-ESOP period. Furthermore the expense associated with the use of perishable tools per sales dollar has also shown improvement, although <u>labor costs</u> per sales dollar has not changed noticeably since the initiation of the ESOP, perhaps because increased productive efficiency is partially compensated by increased pay for those employees who are working on incentives.

Two indices of employee behavior that are relevant to company performance, the rate of grievances and the turnover rate of salaried employees[1], have also shown favorable change since the ESOP was installed, but absenteeism and accident rates have not changed one way or the other.

---

[1] Data concerning non-salaried employees are unavailable from company records.

The available measure of absenteeism may be problematic, however, since it is based on person-days lost rather than on the number of absences that have occurred. The former is heavily influenced by a few persons who have serious long term illnesses and it is not sufficiently sensitive to the effect of "problem" employees who are absent often but for very short periods of time. Data concerning the latter type of absenteeism are not available in the records.

Conclusion

The company appears to have experienced a recovery in recent years according to a number of attitudinal, behavioral, and economic indicators. It is not possible in this preliminary analysis, however, to provide a definitive explanation of this recovery or to attach specific weight to the ownership plan itself. Some of the data do indicate that the plan is having positive effects, both direct and indirect. Yet the company has operated during earlier periods (prior to 1969) at levels of profitability as high if not higher than current levels. Furthermore, we can not say on the basis of this limited analysis that the company is performing better (or worse) than other, traditionally owned companies in its industry.

Perhaps the most unequivocal support for the effectiveness of the plan comes from the employees themselves, who indicate through interviews an unusually high level of morale, motivation, and commitment to the success of the company. The transition to employee ownership is not yet complete (the passing on of voting rights is scheduled to occur in several years) and the effects of employee ownership whether positive or negative are therefore not yet fully realized. Nonetheless, given the very positive attitudinal and motivational climate, and the demonstrable success of the company at present, there is reason to expect that performance will continue at present levels at least, barring a serious decline in the market for the company's product.

DATE DUE		
FEB 15 1983 TERM		
MAY 31 1983 TERM		
MAY 31 1984 TERM		
FEB 15 1986 Term		
IL: 5898264 2/20/88		
NOV 15 1988		
Repair 9-19-89		
OCT 2 1989		